Cambridge **Discovery** E

► **INTERACTIVE READERS**

Series editor: Bob Hastings

SUGAR
OUR GUILTY PLEASURE

A2+

Theo Walker

Distributed By:
Grass Roots Press   wn,
Toll Free: 1-888-303-3213
Fax: (780) 413-6582
Web Site: www.grassrootsbooks.net
                                         '3, USA

www.cambridge.org
Information on this title: www.cambridge.org/9781107681460

First published 2014

Printed in Hong Kong, China, by Golden Cup Printing Company Limited

A catalog record for this publication is available from the British Library.

Library of Congress Cataloging-in-Publication Data

Walker, Theo.
  Sugar : our guilty pleasure / Theo Walker.
    pages cm. -- (Cambridge discovery interactive readers)
  ISBN 978-1-107-68146-0 (pbk. : alk. paper)
  1. Sugar--Juvenile literature. 2. English language--Textbooks for foreign speakers. 3. Readers (Elementary) I. Title.

TP378.2.W35 2013
664'.1--dc23

                      2013016888

ISBN 978-1-107-68146-0

Additional resources for this publication at www.cambridge.org

Layout services, art direction, book design, and photo research: Q2ABillSMITH GROUP
Editorial services: Hyphen S.A.
Audio production: CityVox, New York
Video production: Q2ABillSMITH GROUP

Contents

Before You Read: Get Ready!

Do you like to eat sweet things? Most people do. Sweeteners can be made from a few different kinds of plants, but the most popular sweetener today is sugar. Read on to learn about our long history with – and dangerous love of – sugar.

Words to Know

Read the paragraph and label the pictures with the correct highlighted words.

1. _____

2. _____

3. _____

4. _____

5. _____

Do you know where sugar comes from? Today, most sugar comes from a plant called sugar cane. A farmer grows sugar cane on a very large farm called a plantation. When the juice of the sugar cane is cooked, it becomes black, thick, and very sweet. This is called molasses. The molasses goes to the factory where the white sugar is taken out. This white sugar is also called refined sugar. Refined sugar and other sugars are very popular ingredients in many foods today, and not just cakes and cookies. You can find sugar in almost everything!

Read the paragraph. Then complete the sentences with the correct forms of the highlighted words.

In 1492, Christopher Columbus sailed west from Spain to the Caribbean. He came to some islands which he called the West Indies. There were native people living there, but Columbus said that the islands were now a colony of Spain. In the years that followed, Europeans made many colonies in "the New World." They built plantations and grew crops. They traded these crops for things from Europe. They needed many workers for the plantations. So they bought people, called slaves, to work on the plantations for no money. The colonies caused many changes in history and in the lives of many people.

1 _____ are plants that people grow on farms.

2 _____ were people who were bought by other people.

3 A _____ is a place in another country where Europeans lived and worked.

4 _____ are the first people to live in a country or area.

5 When you _____ something, you make something happen.

6 When you _____ things, you buy something and sell something else.

(?)

PREDICT

Where did the slaves who worked in the fields come from? How did the Europeans bring them to the New World?

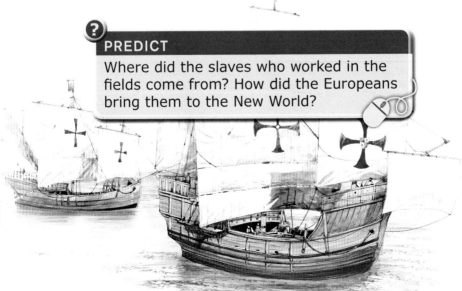

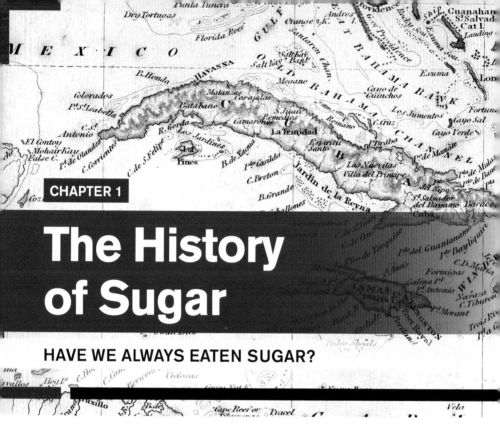

CHAPTER 1

The History of Sugar

HAVE WE ALWAYS EATEN SUGAR?

Today, people eat a lot of sugar. It is easy for most people to buy sweet things and to cook with sugar. It is part of our daily lives.

But sugar has not always been so easy to get. 300 years ago it was unusual for people to have sugar. Where did sugar come from and what is its history? How has the sugar business changed the world?

The first sugar cane grew on the island of New Guinea around 6000 BCE. Around 1000 BCE, sugar cane was brought in boats to India. People first chewed[1] sugar cane because they knew that a very sweet juice came out. It **tasted** good!

---

[1] **chew:** break pieces of food with the teeth

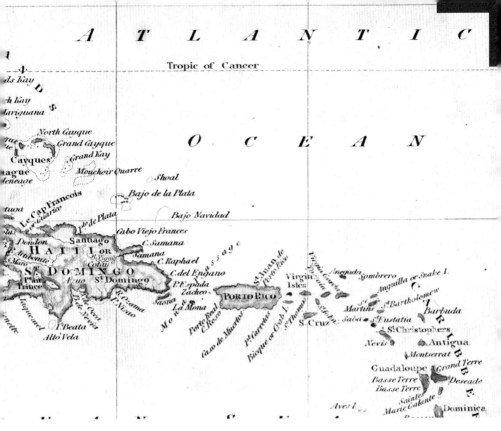

People soon learned how to take the juice out of the cane. They cooked the cane in water, dried it, and were left with small pieces of sugar, called crystals.

In the 8th century CE, Arabs brought sugar cane to Spain. When Columbus went to the West Indies for the second time, in 1493, he took a sugar cane plant with him. The weather there, with lots of sun and rain, was excellent for growing sugar cane.

The weather in the southern United States was also excellent for growing sugar cane. By the 18th century, farmers there were growing sugar cane on plantations. But sugar was expensive because making sugar from cane was not fast or easy. People used it as a spice,[2] like cinnamon, curry, or ginger, not as a main ingredient.

In 1879, in California, a new factory found a way to make sugar faster and cheaper. The plantation owners and the factory owners were making a

Sugar factory, Louisiana, 1900

lot of money because sugar was cheaper to make and people were buying a lot of it. Making sugar became an important business. By 1900, there were more than 30 sugar factories in the United States. Suddenly there was a lot more sugar in the shops.

---

[2]**spice:** plants or parts of plants used in cooking to make food taste more interesting. Cinnamon, curry, and ginger are examples of spices.

In 1700, the average American ate less than two kilos of sugar a year. But as sugar became cheaper and easier to buy, people in Europe and the United States ate much more of it. They started to drink their tea and coffee sweetened with sugar. They started to eat more chocolate, jams, and candies made with sugar. By 1900, the average American ate over 30 kilos of sugar a year!

Sugar has not only changed what people eat and drink. The big business of growing sugar cane and making sugar has also changed the history of several countries. Sometimes these changes have been good, and sometimes the changes have been very bad.

Video Quest

Treats

Watch this video to find out about people's favorite special foods, or treats. Which treats are not sweet?

CHAPTER 2

The Colonies

HOW THE EUROPEAN COLONIES CHANGED THE WORLD.

As sugar became more popular, Europeans wanted to grow as much of it as possible and sell it in Europe. By the 17th century, there were many new sugar plantations in colonies all over the world.

The island group of Hawaii in the Pacific Ocean is a good example of what happened in the colonies.

Hawaii is an excellent place for growing sugar cane. When Captain Cook went to Hawaii in 1778, he was surprised to see **native** people growing sugar cane on small farms. In 1835, an American company started the first large sugar cane plantation in Hawaii. It made a lot of money so other American companies built plantations there also. In 1937, a factory to make refined sugar from the cane was built.

? EVALUATE

Why do you think the Europeans did not work on the sugar plantations? Why did the native people have to do the work?

The Hawaiian Islands are an excellent place to grow sugar cane.

The sugar business changed Hawaii in many ways. The sugar companies took the best land for the plantations. They did not pay the workers very much money, and the hours of work were very long. Many people died from the hard work and new diseases.[3] Life became very difficult for the native Hawaiians.

Life became even worse after a law[4] was passed in 1848. The law said that foreigners could buy land in Hawaii. By 1890, much of Hawaii belonged to foreigners. The sugar companies needed more workers, so they brought people to Hawaii from China, Japan, Korea, and other countries.

Being a **colony** brought many problems to the people working on plantations in Hawaii and other places. But the worst problem was **slavery**.

[3]**disease:** a bad sickness; you can get some diseases from other people
[4]**law:** what a country says you can or must do

CHAPTER 3

Sugar and Slaves

HOW DID SUGAR BECOME PART OF THE BIG BUSINESS OF BUYING AND SELLING SLAVES?

The colonies in the West Indies and America needed workers for the plantations. Europeans and Americans wanted **slaves** to do the work so they didn't have to pay them. They **traded** things like guns and cloth for the slaves.

The slaves were African people who were caught, sold, and then sent to the southeastern United States and to the West Indies to work on sugar and cotton[5] plantations.

[5]**cotton:** a plant used to make cloth for clothes

The ships were filled with as many slaves as possible. Many of them died during the journey. From 1492 to about 1850, 12 million Africans became slaves and were taken to North and South America. Two million of them died before they got there.

The slaves were traded to the plantations for sugar, molasses, and cotton. These things were then taken to the northern United States and to Europe. In factories there, rum[6] was made from molasses, and cloth was made from cotton. With the money made from selling these things, more slaves were bought in Africa and sold in the plantations.

This business between Europe, Africa, the West Indies, and the United States was called the "triangle[7] trade". From the end of the 16th century to the middle of the 19th century, Europeans and Americans made a lot of money from the triangle trade, but it was terrible for the African people.

[6]**rum:** a drink made from molasses
[7]**triangle:** something that has three sides

Businessmen traded guns for slaves.

The Africans, of course, did not want to live like slaves. In 1733 on the Danish island of St. John in the West Indies, some slaves decided to become free.

On the night of November 23, 1733, the slaves killed many of the Danish, Dutch, and French colonists on St. John. Most of the colonists had to leave the island.

For many months the slaves were free. But in April 1734, the French came from the island of Martinique to help the Danish fight the slaves. In August 1734 all the slaves were caught or killed.

More than a hundred years later, in 1848, the African slaves on St. John finally became free.

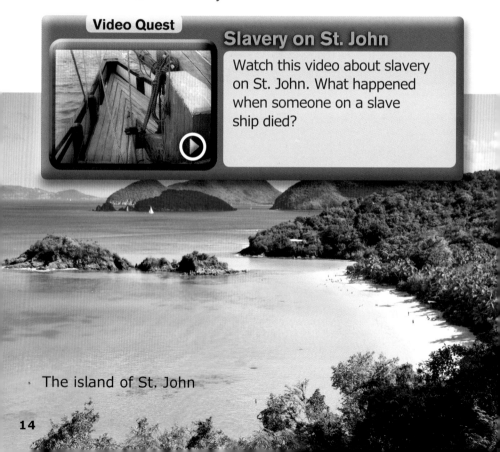

Video Quest

Slavery on St. John

Watch this video about slavery on St. John. What happened when someone on a slave ship died?

The island of St. John

The triangle trade changed the history of the world. Africa lost 12 million people. Many families were broken apart when people were taken from their homes to be slaves. Europe made a lot of money, which helped make the Industrial Revolution.[8] And the arrival of the African slaves changed the people, the culture, and the music of America.

The triangle trade also changed the history of the British colonies in North America. In 1764 these colonies had to pay a tax[9] to Britain for sugar from the West Indies. The colonists did not want to pay the tax, so they decided to become free from Britain. In 1776, 13 of these colonies became the United States of America.

[8] **Industrial Revolution:** the time in history when people started to work in factories

[9] **tax:** money that you must pay to your country when you buy things

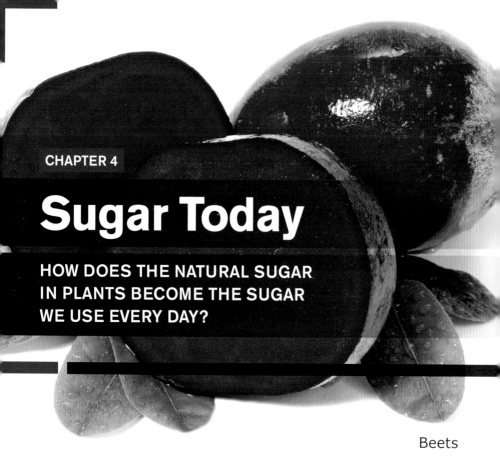

CHAPTER 4

Sugar Today

HOW DOES THE NATURAL SUGAR IN PLANTS BECOME THE SUGAR WE USE EVERY DAY?

Beets

All fruits and some vegetables, like sugar cane, corn, and beets, have natural sugar. When this natural sugar is taken out of the plant in a factory, it is called refined sugar. But exactly how does natural sugar become refined sugar?

Let's look at sugar cane. First, the cane is cut and broken into small pieces. This makes juice come out of the cane. As the juice is cooked, sugar crystals can be seen in the molasses. When the crystals are cleaned, we have white refined sugar. Molasses has things in it that are very good for our health, but refined sugar does not.

Today, 80 percent of the sugar people use comes from sugar cane. Brazil is now the largest grower of sugar cane in the world.

But Brazilians do not only eat sugar. They also make ethanol with it. Ethanol is used in cars and other machines instead of gas. Cars can use as much as 85 percent ethanol and only 15 percent gas. Today, ethanol is used more than gas in Brazil.

In colder countries, like France, the sugar beet is grown for sugar. The United States, however, gets most of its refined sugar from corn. This sugar is used in all kinds of foods. Today, the average American eats about 40 kilos of corn sugar a year.

Corn

Honey is a natural sweetener made by bees.

Today, people who want to be healthy are using other kinds of natural **sweeteners** to make food taste sweet. A good example is honey.

Honey is a natural sweetener that people have used for thousands of years. Bees get juice, called nectar, from flowers to make honey. To make one kilo of honey, bees fly more than 175,000 kilometers and get the juice from more than four million flowers! Many people all over the world use honey like a medicine for skin problems and sicknesses like colds.

Today, science can make **artificial** sweeteners in factories. Refined sugar and natural sugars can cause health problems for people. They can also cause people to gain weight.[10] So, people who don't want to eat or drink sugar can use artificial sweeteners.

[10]**gain weight:** become heavier in your body

Two kinds of artificial sweeteners are saccharine and aspartame. Saccharine is about 500 times sweeter than sugar, and aspartame is 200 times sweeter!

These artificial sweeteners are in a lot of the food that people eat today. For example, many soft drinks now use artificial sweeteners. These soft drinks are sometimes called "lite" or "diet" drinks to show that they don't have sugar in them. But artificial sweeteners may be more dangerous than sugar. Some doctors think that artificial sweeteners can cause big health problems.

(?) APPLY

Think about the things you eat and drink all the time. Do any of those foods or drinks use artificial sweeteners instead of sugar? Why do you choose them?

CHAPTER 5

Sweet But Dangerous

WHAT ARE THE DANGERS OF EATING TOO MUCH SUGAR?

We all know that too much sugar can hurt your teeth and cause you to gain weight. Being too heavy can cause health problems, such as **diabetes**. Today, the average person eats about 21 kilos of sugar each year, which is definitely too much!

We know we eat too much sugar, so why don't we stop? Perhaps it is because many of us crave sugar, or want it so much that we think we need it. Some doctors think people crave sugar because the milk that babies get from their mothers' bodies is sweet. So, when we eat sweet things, we feel comfortable and safe.

Today, too many people in the world are obese, or much too heavy. In the past 20 years, many more people have become obese. In the United States, about 36 percent of adults and 17 percent of children are obese. Is this because they eat too much sugar?

Sugar is a big part of the problem, but there are other reasons that people are obese. One reason is that people don't get enough exercise. In the past, people played more games and sports. They took walks or went dancing. Now that we have TV and computers, many people sit for hours without moving. So they eat too much sugar, and they don't get enough exercise.

Video Quest

Childhood Obesity

Watch this video to find out three reasons why children in the United States are more obese than in the past.

Type 2 diabetes can be caused by eating badly for a long time.

The biggest problem with eating too much sugar may be that it can cause a disease called type 2 diabetes. Type 1 diabetes is natural – a person is born with it. In type 1 diabetes, the body cannot use its own glucose, or blood sugar. Type 2 diabetes, however, is not natural. People get this disease from eating badly for many years.

In the past, very few people had type 2 diabetes. But by 2012, 346 million people in the world had it. It's a very serious disease. It can hurt your heart and your blood. You can lose the use of your eyes, feet, or legs. People with diabetes often die sooner than people without it. Fortunately, for most people, healthy eating and enough exercise will stop type 2 diabetes.

How can we stop eating so much sugar when it is an ingredient in so many things that we eat and drink?

For example, a soft drink can have 39 grams of sugar – that's about 13 teaspoons. Doctors say that drinking only one soft drink a day makes it twice as possible that a person will get diabetes.

Another problem is that there is a lot of sugar in some foods that are not sweet, like bread and cold meats. A can of soup may have as much as 30 grams of sugar in it. So you can get too much sugar without eating dessert!

If you get plenty of exercise and choose with care what you eat and drink, you can stay healthy in a world full of sugar. Remember, with sugar, less is better!

CHAPTER 6

What Do You Think?

SHOULD THERE BE LAWS ABOUT SUGAR?

We now know that eating too much sugar can be dangerous, and that too many people in the world are obese. Many people die of diabetes and other diseases that are caused by obesity every year. In fact, every ten seconds somewhere in the world one person dies from diabetes. This is a very serious health problem.

Today people in many countries are discussing ways to stop people from eating so much sugar. Some people think that countries should make laws for their people about how much sugar is safe to eat. Other people don't agree. They think that each person should be able to choose how much sugar to eat.

A warning label tells people that something is dangerous.

France, Hungary, and Finland are countries where there are now taxes on foods with a lot of sugar, like soft drinks. Do you think making these foods more expensive will stop people from eating too much sugar?

Some people want to put warning labels on foods that have a lot of sugar. The label will tell people that the food is dangerous to their health.

But some people think that we don't need warning labels. These people think that we only need to teach people more about the dangers of eating too much sugar. What do you think?

After You Read

Read the following sentences and choose Ⓐ (True),
Ⓑ (False), or Ⓒ (Doesn't say).

❶ In 1700, the average person ate 24 kilograms of sugar a year.

  Ⓐ True
  Ⓑ False
  Ⓒ Doesn't say

❷ People sometimes traded cotton cloth for slaves in colonial times.

  Ⓐ True
  Ⓑ False
  Ⓒ Doesn't say

❸ There is a lot of sugar in pizza.

  Ⓐ True
  Ⓑ False
  Ⓒ Doesn't say

❹ Slavery helped make the Industrial Revolution.

  Ⓐ True
  Ⓑ False
  Ⓒ Doesn't say

❺ In Brazil, more sugar is made into ethanol than is eaten each year.

  Ⓐ True
  Ⓑ False
  Ⓒ Doesn't say

❻ Honey is an example of an artificial sweetener.

  Ⓐ True
  Ⓑ False
  Ⓒ Doesn't say

7 Just one soft drink can have 39 grams of sugar.

  Ⓐ True

  Ⓑ False

  Ⓒ Doesn't say

8 Diabetes kills more people than any other disease today.

  Ⓐ True

  Ⓑ False

  Ⓒ Doesn't say

Complete the Sentences

Write the correct name of the island in each space.

1 Sugar cane first grew on the island of _____ around 6000 BCE.

2 In 1493, Columbus brought sugar cane plants to the islands of the _____ .

3 Captain Cook went to _____ in 1778.

4 The island where the slaves fought to be free in 1733 is called _____ .

Your Opinion

How can we stop people from eating too much sugar? Write your ideas.

_____

_____

_____

_____

_____

_____

Answer Key

Words to Know, page 4
1 ingredients **2** plantation **3** molasses
4 sugar cane **5** refined sugar

Words to Know, page 5
1 Crops **2** Slaves **3** colony **4** Native people
5 cause **6** trade

Predict, page 5
Answers will vary.

Video Quest, page 9
Lasagna and broccoli.

Evaluate, page 11
Answers will vary.

Video Quest, page 14
When someone died on the ship, they threw the body over
the side into the ocean, where sharks were waiting to eat it.

Apply, page 19
Answers will vary.

Video Quest, page 21
1 Many foods today have a lot of fat and sugar. **2** Children
are less active. **3** Families don't eat together as much and
foods outside of the home are not as healthy.

True or False, page 26
1 B **2** A **3** C **4** A **5** C **6** B **7** A **8** C

Complete the Sentences, page 27
1 New Guinea **2** West Indies **3** Hawaii **4** St. John

Your Opinion, page 27
Answers will vary.